NURSING HOME FEARS

A BUYER'S GUIDE TO LONG-TERM CARE INSURANCE

KEN R. BUTLER

Copyright © 2014 Ken R. Butler
All rights reserved.

ISBN: 1494918854
ISBN 13: 9781494918859
Library of Congress Control Number: 2014900449
CreateSpace Independent Publishing Platform
North Charleston, South Carolina

*Dedicated to Shirley Smith, my mother-in-law,
and Bob Butler, my father. Both suffered from Alzheimer's.
Ten percent of the proceeds of this book will be donated
to the national Alzheimer's Association.*

TABLE OF CONTENTS

Foreword ··· ix

Introduction—What Are Common Consumer Concerns? ··· xi

What Are the Common Myths about Long-Term
Care Insurance? ····································· 1

Do You Need Long-Term Care Insurance? ·············· 5

- Purchase If Adjusted Net Worth Is $100,000 or Less? ··· 8
- Long-Term Care Insurance Survey ················ 9
- Do Not Overlook Veterans' Long-Term
  Care Benefits ································· 11

What Is a Fair Price for LTC Insurance? ················ 13

- Determining a Fair Price for Long-Term
  Care Insurance ································ 14

Common Exclusions and Restrictions
That May Block Claim Recovery ····················· 17

What Options/Benefits Make Comparison Difficult? 21

- Jack's Story 21

How Much Insurance to Purchase? 27

Should a Qualified or Nonqualified
Policy Be Purchased? 31

What Is a "Partnership" Long-Term Care Policy? 33

How Much Insurance Do Other People Purchase? 35

Should an LTC Policy Be Used to Bridge
Medicare Eligibility Planning? 37

A Personal Case Study—Claim Frustrations 41

2014: Will the Affordable Care Act
Change Long-Term Health Care? 43

Is There a Future for Long-Term
Care Insurance in 2014 and Beyond? 45

- Why Plan? Just Rely on Medicaid. 46
- What Are the Eligibility Tests for Medicaid? 46

Can Life Insurance Offset the Cost of Long-Term Care? ... 49

- The 1035 Exchange 50
- Long-Term Care Benefit Plan 51

What Happens When the Money Runs Out? 55

Conclusion · 57

References · 59

Supplement A: Long-Term Care
Insurance Policy Comparison Worksheet · · · · · · · · · · · · · · 61

About the Author · 67

FOREWORD

Nothing is more bewildering than trying to build a defense against events yet to come. Deciding whether or not to purchase long-term care (LTC) insurance is just as perplexing. How do I know? My wife and I have spent the last twenty years discussing this issue, going over the pros and cons, back and forth, up and down, without being able to pull the trigger and purchase a policy.

We knew that the longer we waited to purchase LTC, the more expensive it would be because of our increasing ages. But it only added to our anxiety to know that our inaction would ultimately cost us dearly if we decided to buy LTC at much older ages.

As baby boomers born in the early 1940s, my wife and I began to see many examples of reasons not to purchase LTC—friends and relatives who dropped dead and never spent a day in the hospital—as well as reasons to take out a policy—parents and friends who required expensive extended care, which drained a lifetime of savings.

We remained frozen in this quandary, and I am not sure that we would have ever decided one way or the other. But then I received a request from a friend, Ken Butler, who has a risk management company, to read his manuscript and decide if I would be willing to write the foreword for the book. He had heard me mention my inability to decide on the value of LTC. So that and his experiences with his parents prompted him to write *this book*.

KEN R. BUTLER

I opened the well-written, easy-to-read, fact-filled manuscript and almost immediately began to smile. I began to see answers to the questions that had plagued us for years. Butler does not sell any insurance products—he works only for the consumer. His company, Legacy Risk Solutions, LLC, is independent and objective, so I had no reason to fear that the information he presented would be anything but factual.

As I read on, I continued to smile because the book so clearly presents a list of questions, the answers to which give you direction in making a decision. And since each person and his or her circumstances are different, the reader can deduce the best situation based on the information provided.

Near the beginning of this buyer's guide, Butler allows you to answer the question of whether or not you need long-term care insurance. You decide by taking a simple survey. At the end of the assessment, depending on how you responded to a set of questions, you should know whether or not you are a candidate for LTC insurance. Simple.

If you are a candidate, Butler even gives you parameters for determining how much insurance to purchase. If you are not a contender, then you will know how to proceed.

After Sharon and I read the book, we quickly and easily made a decision. So, now we have one less thing to worry about—probably adding more productive time to our lives now that this worrisome issue has finally been laid to rest.

Robert H. Jordan Jr.

Robert H. Jordan Jr, PhD, is a reporter and anchor with WGN Television in Chicago. He is also the founder and CEO of Jordan & Jordan Communications, Inc. (http://videofamilybiographies.com). His company produces luxury, documentary-style video biographies for high-net-worth families across the country. J&J also works with private equity firms to provide marketing expertise and video profiles of newly acquired companies. Mr. Jordan can be contacted at robert.jordan@aol.com.

INTRODUCTION— WHAT ARE COMMON CONSUMER CONCERNS?

It seems everyone is trying to sell long-term care insurance! Insurance agents, banks, financial planning consultants, associations like AARP, and even companies involved in direct sales efforts over the Internet have all gotten into the act, which is a good indication that there is money to be made selling this product. The long-term care products are intentionally marketed using glossy brochures, with so many options that it makes a fair comparison *nearly impossible* for the consumer. Consumer concerns include:

1. Is the insurance company financially stable?

2. What is the likelihood an insurance company will raise rates in the first three years?

3. How can the buyer force a fair comparison?

4. Which options are the most important?

5. What tricks do insurance companies use to limit access to benefits?

6. Does the insurance make sense for the buyer's needs and wealth profile?

A common complaint is that insurance companies increase rates three and four times from the time of purchase! This situation has not changed for the insurance companies; insurers retain the right to increase rates on all new policies if raised for all age-classes.

> Long-term care insurance is a wise purchase for some but *not all consumers.*

Long-term care insurance is a wise purchase for some but *not all consumers.* However, this insurance product has been a *win-win for the insurance industry!* Long-term care insurance products have been sold since the early 1990s. Many consumers who bought these early policies were told that purchasing the policies at an early age, well in advance of retirement, would *lock in the rates.* Unfortunately, consumers were not clearly informed that the insurance companies reserved their right to increase future rates *if the insurance company increased the rates for all their policyholders within the same age-class.*

This buyer's guide will provide answers to the above-mentioned consumer concerns. This guide has been developed by Legacy Risk Solutions, an independent risk management company that *does not sell insurance products.* LRS only works for the consumer in order to maintain *independence and objectivity.* The guide will help the buyer to evaluate proposals using a comparison worksheet that forces a fair comparison.

WHAT ARE THE COMMON MYTHS ABOUT LONG-TERM CARE INSURANCE?

What are the odds of ending up in a nursing home?

The aggressive sales tactics used by some insurance agents have led to overstated statistics to create fear and apprehension. For example, when you type "What is the probability of going into a nursing home?" into Google, there is a wide range of responses! I discovered stated averages as high as 60 percent! In fact, as noted in the article "The Nursing Home Dilemma," the average is closer to 40 percent, with far more women needing care—52 percent versus 33 percent of men.[1] The reason for the difference? Women live longer.

Other common myths include:

---

[1] James C. Skeeles, "The Nursing Home Dilemma," publication no. EP 10–12, Ohio State Extension Community Development Fact Sheet (Columbus, OH: Ohio State, 2012).

1. **"You can pay for long-term care insurance without any out-of-pocket expenses!"** Be wary of any salesperson suggesting that you pay for long-term care insurance by borrowing from your life insurance policy cash value or a retirement plan. In fact, borrowing from any retirement plan or life insurance cash value is perilous. A financial crisis can arise years later, as the interest of the loan compounds, reducing the retirement funds or eroding the cash value to a point that terminates the life insurance policy.

2. **"Buying long-term care insurance is a good investment!"** Long-term care insurance is not an investment. It is a supplemental income policy that reimburses the insured person for expenses, *after* the expenses have been incurred. Some insurance agents link the investment comment with the return-of-premium benefit found in many policies. What a good deal this appears to be! You pay for something, find you never need it, and then your estate receives all your money back after you die!

> [Caution: The policy language is not as certain as it first appears. William Baldwin, in his *Forbes* article, "Dodge the Long-Term Care Insurance Mess," points out the LTC policy permits the insurance company to change the terms after you have put money into the policy. "Imagine buying a Lexus for $5,000 down plus $500 a month under a contract that allows the dealer to raise the payment if he wants to…to $800 per month."[2]]

---

2 William Baldwin, "Dodge the Long Term Care Insurance Mess," *Forbes, The Best Life* (blog), February 20, 2013, http://www.forbes.com/sites/baldwin/2013/03/29/dodge-the-long-term-care-insurance-mess/.

NURSING HOME FEARS

> [***Recommendation:*** ask the agent to disclose the cost of the return-of-premium benefit and ask that it not be included. If the answer is this benefit is built into the program and cannot be removed, try to find another product that will carve this out, because it adds no real value to the program.]

3. **"The premium will never be less than it is today!"** It is true that the rate is lower when you are fifty than if you wait to purchase at age sixty-five. However, the number of years before long-term care benefits are likely to be provided may make the early purchase more expensive!

4. **"You can save money by purchasing a shared policy for a married couple."** In fact, a shared couple policy is more expensive than a single policy for the spouse most likely to need long-term care: the woman. As cited earlier, 52 percent of women and only 33 percent of men will require some long-term care before death.

5. **"Buy the LTC policy when you are young. Health problems later in life could result in a denial of coverage."** It is true that a diagnosis of dementia or Alzheimer's will likely result in the denial of coverage. However, most other health problems can be accepted by factoring the health issues into the rate for the policy. The preexisting condition clause is another way for the insurer to provide a policy, even if the person suffers from chronic illness, such as diabetes.

DO YOU NEED LONG-TERM CARE INSURANCE?

The story about Annie and Bill in the next section illustrates that long-term care insurance is not for everyone. For some, it could be the worst purchase they ever made. An excellent book by Phyllis R. Shelton, *Long-Term Care: Your Financial Planning Guide,* suggests that anyone with assets of between $50,000 and $2,000,000, excluding their home and cars, should seriously consider the coverage. In other words, if your assets are under $50,000 or over $2,000,000, long-term care insurance is not a wise purchase.

It is my opinion this formula is too narrow for the varied circumstances that can arise when extended-care services are needed. Also, I think using assets alone is misleading. The formula should also deduct tax liabilities and annuity surrender surcharges. Therefore, the following formula refers to adjusted net worth, less the equity in your home and vehicles as well as a reduction for the estimated ordinary income tax that is payable on any distributions from qualified retirement plans.

Formula: Net worth
– (Less equity in home and cars)
– (Less tax of qualified plans [IRA, 401(k)])
– (Less annuity or life insurance cash surrender charges)
= Adjusted net worth

> **At best, long-term care insurance is a zero-sum game for most buyers.**

At best, long-term care insurance is a zero-sum game for most buyers. The policies rarely return benefits equal to or greater than the premiums paid after considering the time value of money. Also, there are built-in limit caps (discussed below) that keep this from being a big win for the buyer.

From a financial planning perspective, *one good reason to purchase a long-term care insurance product is to spread out the cost of long-term health costs,* thereby reducing the impact of surrender charges and taxes from forced liquidation of various retirement planning accounts.

- Surprise! Every dollar that has been invested in a 401(k) or an IRA is subject to ordinary income tax upon distribution. A long-term care insurance policy may be used as a tax-planning tool. The LTC policy reimburses expenses incurred on a monthly basis, preventing forced early distributions from qualified retirement plans.

- Annuity accounts have their own penalty triggers that may become a surprise when there is an immediate need for cash for long-term health care. Generally, a portion of the annuity value is available to the annuitant, penalty free. This penalty-free money can be as much as 50 percent of the original premium that was paid for the annuity. After the account holder passes this 50 percent trigger point, surrender charges can be significant and can quickly erode the annuity's value.

[***Observation:*** generally, someone who has an adjusted net worth of more than $100,000 and less than $2,000,000 is likely to have a mix of qualified plans and annuities. The long-term care insurance policy can be an efficient way to spread out the expense as it is incurred, reducing the amount of money that must be withdrawn from qualified plans, and therefore reducing the amount of ordinary income tax that is triggered.] ***Observation:*** people with an adjusted net worth of $100,000 or less will not see much benefit from a long-term care insurance policy for several reasons:

- Their working income would likely have been insufficient to be able to afford the level of long-term care benefit that would be needed to provide a true supplement to their retirement planning.

- The cost of nursing home and expanded assisted living services, at $7,000 to $10,000 per month, would quickly deplete an adjusted net worth less than $100,000, even if the person were to purchase a $100-per-day benefit level.

Take the survey on the next page and find out if you should purchase long-term care insurance.

Purchase If Adjusted Net Worth Is $100,000 or Less?

Annie and Bill were sixty-five and worried that their modest adjusted net worth of $125,000 would not pass to their grandchildren if they ended up in a nursing home. Their monthly income from all sources was $3,000 per month, just enough to meet their monthly expenses. An insurance agent had recommended a long-term care policy that would pay $100 per day benefit, $3,000 per month, for a monthly premium of $200. They decided they could not afford the premium. Their outcome follows:

- Bill eventually entered a nursing home at age eight-six, and stayed there for twenty-four months before his death. If they had purchased the coverage at age sixty-five, assuming no increased premiums over the twenty-one-year period, they would have spent $50,400.

- The care expense for the twenty-four-month period was $120,000. By the date of Bill's entry into the nursing home, at age eighty-six, the couple's adjusted net worth had declined to $25,000. Bill was declared eligible for Medicaid after 50 percent of the $25,000 was spent down, per Medicaid rules.

- Annie remained in the home during the period that Bill was in the long-term care facility without any forced sale triggered by Bill's care expenses.

- At the time of Bill's death, the estate received a statement from the government for the care expenses that

NURSING HOME FEARS

were paid by Medicaid. Bill's financial interest in the equity of the home, 50 percent, was recoverable by the government, up to the amount of the total expenses that were paid by Medicaid. Annie chose to sell the home. Annie then used her remaining 50 percent of the home's equity and her modest savings to rent an apartment near her children.

Long-Term Care Insurance Survey:

1. Is your current adjusted net worth, either individually or as a couple, excluding your cars, home, and ordinary income tax that would be payable when funds are distributed from an IRA or 401(k) (about a 25 percent reduction), greater than $100,000?

    Yes _____   No _____

    - If the answer is no, long-term care insurance is probably not a wise purchase. If the answer is yes, you need to read this book to avoid the pitfalls and make an informed decision.

2. If the answer to question 1 above is yes, is your adjusted net worth, excluding your cars, home, and ordinary income tax that would be payable when funds are distributed from an IRA or 401(k) (about a 25 percent reduction), in excess of $2,000,000?

    Yes _____   No _____

    - If the answer is yes, long-term care insurance may not be a practical purchase and should only be purchased after reading this book and discussing your specific needs with an objective advisor

3. Are you considering the purchase because you think you have Alzheimer's-like symptoms?

Yes _____   No _____

- If the answer is yes, the medical underwriting required for the application will probably catch this pre-existing condition, and you will be turned down for insurance.

4. Is one of your primary reasons for purchasing long-term care insurance to protect your assets in case you go into a nursing home or require some other form of long-term, in-home health care?

Yes _____   No _____

- Long-term care insurance is probably a wise purchase as long as your adjusted net worth is not less than $100,000 and not more than $2,000,000. This book will help you make a decision by providing direction as to the structure and limits that may be considered.

NURSING HOME FEARS

Do Not Overlook Veterans' Long-Term Care Benefits

The Department of Veterans Affairs provides three types of long-term care benefits that are often overlooked by family members:

- benefits for service-related disabilities

- state veterans' homes

- disability payments, including compensation, pension, and death benefits

Some benefits are also available for the spouse of a veteran.

Many veterans may be eligible for some type of long-term care benefit or subsidy from the Veterans Administration. The first step is to visit the VA website, http://www.va.gov, and complete the survey, "Do You Qualify for VA Health Care?"

Eligibility for the various plans varies, depending upon the veteran's income, and on other factors such as when and how long the veteran served and whether he or she was honorably discharged. However, do not assume that a gross income of up to $5,000 per month automatically disqualifies the applicant! Many types of expenses can be used to reduce the veteran's monthly income to a level that permits eligibility. The key is to complete the survey and paperwork to determine eligibility.

A comprehensive article on this subject has been written by Thomas Day: "Veterans Aid and Attendance Pension Benefit and Long-Term Care Benefits for Veterans," published by the

National Care Planning Council. The article describes the various means-testing formulas and describes the benefits offered within each benefit classification.[3]

---

[3] Thomas Day, "Veterans Aid and Attendance Pension Benefit and Long-Term Care Benefits for Veterans," *National Care Planning Council,* accessed January 12, 2014, http://www.longtermcarelink.net/eldercare/long_term_care_benefits_for_veterans.htm.

WHAT IS A FAIR PRICE FOR LTC INSURANCE?

Most consumers find the cost of long-term care insurance surprisingly expensive. There are several reasons for the high cost:

- The cost of medical care inflation is averaging 9 percent per year.

- LTC premium rates are age banded. The older you are, the more it costs.

- Consumer-friendly regulation has forced the industry to abandon early restrictive policy language. The change to more favorable policy language has also resulted in higher premiums.

> [Caution: if you are still paying premium on a first-generation long-term care policy, a product sold before the year 2000, I recommend that the policy be evaluated by an attorney, accountant, or an independent LTC consultant (not the agent who sold the policy).]

Determining a Fair Price for Long-Term Care Insurance

In my experience, a fair premium, assuming benefits will start to be paid at age 85, should be less than 10 percent of the lifetime maximum benefit. The following example compares premiums paid to age eighty-five, starting at age fifty and at age sixty-eight.

Comparison proposal terms:

- $150 per day with inflation rider (doubles to $300 in twenty years)

- 3 year max benefit ($165,000 doubles to $330,000 in twenty years)

- 90-day elimination period, meaning the number of days the person must wait before benefits will begin.

Annual premium if purchased: at age 50 = **$950**; at age 68 = **$2,688**

NURSING HOME FEARS

Note: Using the number of years to age eighty-five (the projected benefit-trigger age), the formula would be as follows:

Annual premium × number of years to 85 =
Divided by the $330,000 lifetime max

Start @ 50: **$33,250 (35 yrs)** = 10 percent (favorable)

Start @ 68: **$45,696 (17 yrs)** = 13.8 percent (unfavorable)

> ***Recommendation:*** consider the cost favorable if the total premium to age eighty-five is no more than 10 percent of the proposed lifetime maximum benefit. If unfavorable, ask the agent to work on a proposal that does not exceed 10 percent of the lifetime benefit.

COMMON EXCLUSIONS AND RESTRICTIONS THAT MAY BLOCK CLAIM RECOVERY

Exclusionary and restrictive language is not only found in the exclusions' section of the policy form. Other sections of the policy that need to be reviewed include:

1. Benefit limits and period:

    - Benefit limits are often capped. For example, there is a maximum benefit limit, which may be stated in terms of dollars as well as time period, such as five years for all benefits paid regardless of the number of interruptions in the benefit payment period. There is often a secondary limit cap—a lower number, a lower number of days, or both—which is the maximum limit if care is provided on a continuous basis, without interruption.

> **Observation:** ask the agent to confirm how the policy language defines *interruption*. You want to be as certain as possible that if the person is transferred between nursing home, hospital, and home, these events constitute an interruption, and the higher benefit cap would then apply over the life of the policy.

- Benefit period: the average stay in a nursing home is 2.4 years.[4] Keep this in mind as you consider a benefit period. A three-year benefit period, about a thousand days, costs less than a five-year benefit period. (Only 25 percent of residents are in a nursing home for more than three years.)

2. Common exclusions to avoid:

    - Be wary of policies that include brain disorder (such as a stroke), dementia, or Alzheimer exclusions.

    - Watch out for language that excludes future claims from undisclosed health conditions that existed prior to the policy being issued. Some insurance companies reserve the right to void coverage at any time in the future if they can make a connection to a health condition that was not disclosed at the time of the application.

---

4 Thomas Day, "About Nursing Homes," *National Care Planning Council,* accessed January 20, 2014, http://www.longtermcarelink.net/eldercare/nursing_home.htm.

> **Recommendation:** ask the agent to confirm the policy is underwritten at the time of the application, not at the time of a claim.

3. Definitions of policy terms must include:

   - home health care, assisted living, and independent living

   - skilled nursing facility

4. Eligibility trigger for long-term care benefits:

   - The policy should kick in if you have either a cognitive impairment or require assistance with not more than two activities of daily living (ADL). The six ADL capabilities include dressing, toileting, eating, transferring, bathing, and continence. The "Best Practice" insurance policy design model on the comparison spreadsheet, at the end of this guide, supports an insurance recovery if the covered person requires assistance with two of the six ADLs.

> [**Observation:** some insurers will only trigger the benefit if three (3) of the ADLs require assistance.]

> ***Recommendation:*** reject any proposal that does not trigger the benefits at two (2) of the ADLs requiring assistance.

WHAT OPTIONS/ BENEFITS MAKE COMPARISON DIFFICULT?

Jack's Story

Jack had followed his agent's advice and purchased the so-called "best plan." Per the marketing brochure, the plan included:

- a five-year benefit period

- a return-of-premium benefit that gives back the premium to the estate if you never use it

- only a thirty-day waiting period

- waiver of premium

- non-forfeiture—even if rates increase

- waiting-period benefit

- restoration benefit

Fifteen years later, when Jack entered the nursing home, his family realized how limited the "best plan" was in reality. Also, they discovered the cost for the plan was almost double the cost of a standard plan.

The comparison worksheet, Supplement A at the end of this guide, is intended to help you derive a fair comparison of proposals. Therefore, the comparison is based upon a standard program with no options or enhancement benefits. Insurance companies use a value-added marketing strategy, throwing in options and benefits, which makes it difficult to compare policies.

Once the buyer decides which proposal and insurance company is superior, the options and enhancement benefits can be added, each on its own merit. Common options or enhancement benefits include:

1. ***Home health care and assisted living options.*** The government is expected to restrict Medicare and Medicaid Nursing Home cost reimbursements, forcing the cost of nursing facilities to increase. This will drive more consumers to home health care or assisted living care. Therefore, you should consider adding both of these options for optimum benefit recovery.

2. ***Inflation rider option.*** This option provides for a benefit increase of up to 5 percent per year. Caution: the premium is increased as well, which is a way to circumvent whatever rate increase guarantee was included in the sales literature.

NURSING HOME FEARS

> [*Observation:* once the consumer is retired, on a fixed income, an increase of 5 percent of benefit per year may not be affordable. The inflation rider is supported for those purchasing the coverage under their retirement age, when they have a higher income. The inflation rider should be discontinued once the person retires.]

> *Recommendation:* ask your agent to confirm that the inflation rider can be discontinued in the future.

3. *Deductible/elimination period option.* The comparison spreadsheet lists a ninety-day elimination period as best practice. The elimination period is the period of time that must elapse after the coverage triggering event, before benefits are paid. It is also often referred to as the waiting period. Some insurance companies will try to sell a lower elimination period, which increases the premium, because a lower elimination period means there are fewer days to wait before benefits begin to be paid.

> *Recommendation:* a ninety-day elimination period is the most cost efficient. Do not fall into the fear trap used in the marketing materials. The risk that

> you or a loved one will end up needing nursing home care still averages less than 50 percent. For women it is 52 percent and for men 33 percent.[5]

Waiver of premium option. Waiver of premium option is attractive at first glance. This option pays the premium for the long-term care insurance during the time the person is in a nursing home receiving long-term care. The problem is the cost. Given the relatively short average duration of care in a nursing home, three years or less, the monthly premium, often in excess of $500 per year, is excessive for the benefit transferred.

> **Recommendation:** if considering waiver of premium, ask the agent to confirm that the waiver will apply whether the person is receiving long-term care in an assisted living, home care, or hospital environment. The waiver should extend as long as the person is receiving assistance with at least two of the activities of daily living.

4. *Non-forfeiture Option.* This option keeps the policy in force in the event of certain circumstances such as an increase in premium. This option gives the insured the right to keep the premiums the same by reducing the amount of benefit, without having the policy lapse.

---

5 Skeeles, "The Nursing Home Dilemma."

NURSING HOME FEARS

> Recommendation: I do not support this option due to the cost, if the cost is 10–15 percent of higher than the basic premium.

5. *Return of Premium Benefit.* The return of premium benefit is an illusion. It is often explained to the consumer as "free" insurance! In reality, the policy language restricts the return of premium after you die so that your heirs are very unlikely to receive it. The premium is only returned if you die after you have reached the *later of* the policy anniversary date *after* you reached the age of one hundred or the twenty-fifth anniversary year of the policy. Example: A person buys the policy at age seventy-seven and dies at age one hundred. There would be no return of premium because the person died in his or her twenty-third year of the policy.

> *Recommendation:* request the cost of this benefit, and ask that it be deleted.

6. *Waiting period benefit.* Most people will never qualify for the recovery of costs incurred during the waiting period, because it is only paid after one year of recovery with no intervening days of long-term care! This is a typical value-added marketing benefit to make the policy seem to stand above others, but it does not provide a meaningful benefit.

> **Recommendation:** request the cost of this benefit, and ask that it be deleted.

7. ***Restoration Benefit.*** Restoration benefit may be an illusion, because it may only be triggered if the person has been care-free for one year! The sales pitch is that partially used up benefits may be reset if the person incurs no additional medical costs in a nursing home for a period of time, usually a year. In reality, it is rare for a person who was in a nursing home to be able to be care free for a year after leaving the nursing home.

HOW MUCH INSURANCE TO PURCHASE?

The cost of long-term care varies widely throughout the country. According to the Administration on Aging, the average cost in 2010 for care in a nursing care facility, with a semiprivate room, meals, physical therapy, and ADL, Activities of Daily Living, assistance with two of the six ADLs, including medication distribution and management, was $205 per day, $6,235 per month.[6]

> [*Observation:* do not hesitate to partially self-insure the risk! The comparison spreadsheet at the end of the book is set up for a benefit of $150 per day, with a ninety-day elimination period, assuming two ADL assistance services, with a $1,000-per-day continuous benefit maximum and a $1,500-per-day all benefit days maximum. The range of the benefits is $150,000 to $225,000.]

---

6 "How to Pay Costs of Care," US Department of Health & Human Services, accessed January 20, 2014, www.longtermcare.gov/costs-how-to-pay/costs-of-care/.

> **Long-term care insurance should not be considered an investment!**

1. Long-term care insurance (LTCI) is a supplement to ordinary income. *LTCI should not be considered an investment!*

2. Here is an easy formula to determine how much benefit to buy:

   - The annual cost of nursing home care in your community, plus $500 per month spending money, $500 per month medical and drug copays, minus the person's projected annual income, divided by 365 days, equals the daily benefit.

   Illustration: $72,000 annual nursing home cost plus $12,000 spending and copay expenses, minus $48,000 annual income, equals $36,000, divided by 365 days, equals a daily benefit of nearly $100.

+ Nursing home expense	$72,000
+ Living expenses	$6,000
+ Medical supplement copays and deductible	$6,000
– Annual income	($48,000)
= Shortfall	$36,000 ÷ 365 days = $99 per day

> ***Observation:*** if your fixed monthly income is above $9,000 per month, $300 per day, long-term care insurance is probably not a wise purchase.

SHOULD A QUALIFIED OR NONQUALIFIED POLICY BE PURCHASED?

A Qualified Policy means the premiums for the long-term care policy premiums may be deductible, as long as they exceed the IRS approved percent of the person's adjusted gross income. The premiums are treated the same as other non-reimbursed medical expenses, including supplemental Medicare insurance premiums.

Nonqualified means the long-term care policy premiums are not deductible. Nonqualified LTC policies are the most popular because the premiums are generally less and the product is not as regulated as the qualified products.

> [***Observation:*** the nonqualified (nontax-deductible) LTC policy will be the most affordable for most buyers. Buyers are encouraged to discuss the possible advantage of a qualified (tax deductible) product with their tax professional. The key question for the tax professional is whether a Qualified plan is a tax deferred product, meaning the benefits, if benefits are paid, may be subject to tax.] (Call out Box)

There are no coverage advantages to a Qualified plan. Insurance companies tend to charge more for these products due to the elevated level of regulation for products that offer payment on a tax deductible basis.

WHAT IS A "PARTNERSHIP" LONG-TERM CARE POLICY?

The "Qualified Plan" state long-term care partnership program was first tested in 1992 and then expanded as a part of the Deficit Reduction Act of 2005. The program exists in most states. (As of the publishing date, only the states of Mississippi, New Mexico, Utah, Michigan, Hawaii, and Arkansas do not have plans in process.) The program's goal is to provide an incentive for people to purchase long-term care insurance by protecting a portion of their assets when they are seeking eligibility for Medicaid.

The asset protection provided by a partnership policy is dollar for dollar. For every dollar of coverage your long-term care policy provides, your protected assets increase by a dollar, above the maximum $1,500 to $2,000 of assets allowable under Medicaid eligibility rules. The maximum assets that can be protected vary by state. Protection of up to $152,000 of assets is understood to be generally available.

[***Observation:*** the "partnership" policy was included within the legislation due to a lobbying effort by the insurance industry. I have concerns that this "protection" of assets will disappear if the partnership policy lapses or is not renewed by the insurance industry.]

Recommendation: consider a "partnership" policy proposal if you plan to use the LTC policy as a strategy for bridging the eligibility gap for Medicaid benefits. This is described in the next section.

HOW MUCH INSURANCE DO OTHER PEOPLE PURCHASE?

Most people purchase an amount less than the full daily cost of long-term care. According to an article by Philip Moeller in *US News & World Report*, the percentage of customers purchasing the amount of coverage given in the left column is as follows:[7]

$99 or less	7 percent
$100 to $149 per day	36 percent
$150 to $199 per day	34 percent
$200 to $249 per day	18 percent
$250 or more	5 percent

---

7 Philip Moeller, "What You Need to Know about Long-Term Care Insurance," *US News & World Report*, accessed January 20, 2014, www.money.usnews.com/money/blogs/the-best-life/2013/02/20/what-you-need-to-know-about-long-term-care-insurance.

SHOULD AN LTC POLICY BE USED TO BRIDGE MEDICAID ELIGIBILITY PLANNING?

Medicaid is the Federal program that will pay for nursing home expenses when a person has no financial means to pay for care. Each state has very specific guidelines that limit the amount of assets a person retains in order to be eligible for Medicaid benefits. In most states, this range of permitted personal assets is between $1,500 and $2,000.

There are financial professionals who specialize in Medicaid eligibility planning. It is recommended that professional advice be sought before pursuing Medicaid eligibility. Also, you should understand that the strategy of reducing your assets to qualify for Medicaid funding of long-term care is not without controversy.

In simplest terms, this is how the strategy works: a person chooses to gift away all of his or her personal assets, and transfers his or her home into an irrevocable trust, in order to be eligible for his or her state's Medicaid long-term care payment system. Jay Adkisson points out three problems inherent in such an asset transfer strategy. "…First, the Federal Statute governing Medicaid eligibility provides for a "look back" period of 36 months, or in the case of transfers to a trust, 60 months… Second, creditors of the transferor (the parent) might claim that the transfer was fraudulent, in derogation of their rights. Third, the creditors of the transferee (the son or daughter) might claim that the assets have been irrevocably transferred by the parent, and are now available to satisfy their (the creditors) claims."[8]

Other common problems I have observed include:

- children who become divorced, forcing a sale of the house where parents are living. The irrevocable trust is a document that removes the house, the asset, from the parents, placing the house into a trust. Once the irrevocable trust is established, the parent loses all rights to the home. The child usually becomes the beneficiary of the trust. This all works fine unless the son or daughter becomes divorced. The disgruntled son or daughter in law's attorney may decide the beneficiary asset of the trust should now be counted by the courts as one half interest belonging to the child's spouse. If the child does not have the cash to pay off their former spouse, the house may have to be sold!

- disagreements as to who is to pay for the upkeep of the home;

- the quality of the nursing facilities that accept Medicaid patients; and

---

[8] Jay Adkisson, "Asset Protection Planning In Anticipation Of Medicaid Fails In Woodworth Case," *Forbes*, accessed January 20, 2014, www.forbes.com/sites/jayadkisson/2013/02/27/asset-protection-planning-ub-anticipation-of-medicaid-fails-in-woodworth-case/

- the distance loved ones need to travel to visit a facility that will accept Medicaid.

> **Observation:** a strategy sometimes suggested as a part of the sale of Long Term Care insurance is to use the long-term care insurance as a bridge for paying for care during what is now a five-year prior look back period. The IRS uses this look back period to determine if the proposed insured person has gifted assets to someone else, attempting to hide assets by transferring them to another person. Under current law, the government can force the recall (means the government can void the attempted transfer) of the assets that are transferred within five years before the person became eligible and started receiving Medicaid assistance for long-term care benefits.

My prediction is that state governments are all under stress and looking for ways to increase revenue and decrease spending. One way to increase revenue is for the state or the federal government to tax the assets that are stripped away from the government (i.e., gifted) when the purpose is for the owner of the assets to become eligible for Medicaid. Another method the government may employ to reduce eligibility, and thereby reduce spending, is to keep increasing the number of years for asset transfer recall. It used to be a three-prior-year review; now it is a five-prior-year review, and the prior-year review may increase to seven years in the years ahead.

[***Recommendation:*** Medicaid eligibility planning works for the current time in 2014. I am not an advocate of using the LTC insurance policy as a bridge. In my opinion, this creates a false expectation for the buyer that the strategy will still work even if governmental regulations change. The encouragement of this false expectation could lead some buyers to purchase the policy, hoping to save something for their heirs.]

A PERSONAL CASE STUDY—CLAIM FRUSTRATIONS

I wanted to conclude with a real-life story, including the real-life frustrations of dealing with an insurance company twenty years after the policy was purchased and the selling agent was long ago retired or dead!

My family has firsthand experience with the benefits and problems of long-term care insurance. My mother- and father-in-law purchased long-term care insurance at age sixty-five. The original premiums, in 1990, were $250 each, a total of $500 for the year. The insurance company raised the premiums for all policyholders, five times over twenty years, so that the premiums for this married couple had risen to $1,250 total by the time they reached age eighty-five. They paid a total premium of $17,500, up to the time of my mother-in-law's death.

My mother-in-law required long-term care off and on over a period of three years and nine months (3.75 years). Her daily benefit was $60 per day. The maximum continuous benefit in the policy was for a thousand days ($60,000), and the benefit days increased to fifteen hundred days ($90,000) if the care was not continuous.

She died on the 1,277th day after she had satisfied the ninety-day waiting (elimination) period for her benefits to begin. Her long-term care was intermittent over that period (she was in and out of the hospital for a total of ten days over the 3.75-year period), thereby suspending the long-term benefit payments for those ten days. After her death, the family expected total insurance reimbursements to be $75,960 ($60 per day times 1,266 days). Instead, the family received payments only for the thousand-day benefit, for a total payout of $60,000. To date, the insurance company has refused to pay the additional $15,960 for the additional 266 days of benefit. Their stated reason is that they do not recognize the hospital days as interruptions in the long-term health care. It is the insurance company's position that the benefit has been paid in full.

Recommendations:

1. The above frustration may be avoided by purchasing a policy with a single stated maximum benefit period, as shown on the comparison spreadsheet.

2. Buyer beware!

2014: WILL THE AFFORDABLE CARE ACT CHANGE LONG-TERM HEALTH CARE?

According to the American Association for Long-Term Care Insurance, a national industry trade group, consumers have developed several misconceptions about the impact of the Affordable Care Act on long-term care insurance.

The misconceptions include:

- The ACA will require insurance companies to waive pre-existing health conditions. Fact: the ACA does not apply to long-term care insurance. All LTC insurance companies will continue to require health screening as a part of the application process.

- Long-term care insurance companies are required to pay all costs related to long-term care, without any lifetime caps. Fact: most long-term care insurance policies issued after 2005 have a maximum lifetime benefit. This will not change in 2014.

- The ACA will expand Medicare to pay for long-term care benefits. Fact: the ACA has no provisions that will change Medicare so that it pays for long-term care benefits.

Some of the misunderstandings among consumers are due to the expectations that have been raised by the political debate. While a congressional commission has been formed to examine all elements of the Affordable Care Act, there is no guarantee that any changes will come from the report.

Jesse Sloan, the executive director of the American Association for Long-Term Care Insurance, suggested in a 2013 article, "Long-Term Care Insurance Is Not Changed by Obama Care," that the debate will likely be focused on cutting back Medicare and Medicaid expenditures during the 2016 presidential campaigns.[9]

The rules of Medicaid are likely to change in the future. The regulatory "look back" periods, which determine proper asset transfers, will likely become longer, so that early planning for retirement will become even more important. In my opinion, the need for long-term care insurance for those of modest wealth will continue to be an important planning tool, regardless of the future changes that might be made to the Affordable Care Act.

---

9 Jesse Sloan, "Long-Term Care Insurance Is Not Changed by Obamacare," American Association for Long-Term Care Insurance, accessed January 20, 2014, www.aaltci.org/news/long-term-care-insurance-is-not-changed-by-obamacare.

IS THERE A FUTURE FOR LONG-TERM CARE INSURANCE IN 2014 AND BEYOND?

There are two sobering thoughts as 2014 begins, summarized by Keith R. Fevurly, MBA, JD, LLM, CFP, in an article in the *Financial Professionals Journal of Financial Services Professionals*:[10]

- The majority of American families today have no plan for paying for nursing home care. It has been estimated that 64 percent of all current nursing home residents are funded by Medicaid.

- The ongoing low-interest-rate environment is likely to continue through 2015. Long-term care insurance costs are negatively impacted by a low-interest-rate environment because insurance companies are unable to receive

---

10 Keith R. Fevurly, "Alternatives to Long-Term Care Insurance," *Journal of Financial Service Professionals* 66, no. 6: 61–68 (2012), http://search.ebscohost.com/login.aspx?direct=true&profile=ehost&scope=site&authtype=crawler&jrnl=15371816&AN=83233390&h=NKeUaYcPGksStAc4%2BSCKLNtkpKv764WBF33eoqd4D%2BRsvrAWKbxMiDhSK%2B%2BvKCHFbeFIbgmmrBeWO3sIaRIQew%3D%3D&crl=c.

an acceptable return on investments. Long-term care insurance companies have already taken steps to improve the profitability of the product by increasing rates and reducing eligibility. Also, some insurance companies are choosing to abandon the product altogether.

Why Plan? Just Rely on Medicaid.

Medicaid has become the preferred alternative for funding nursing home care because of favorable eligibility requirements and, until recently, little or no effort from the government to recover the expense of the care provided. It is believed that within the next four years, eligibility will be tightened, copays will be pushed down to the consumer, and recovery of expenses will be made a priority at both the state and federal level.

What Are the Eligibility Tests for Medicaid?

The federal government establishes the eligibility rules, and then the states are left to manage their Medicaid program within the rules. Generally, the asset test in most states is that the prospective recipient of Medicaid must not have total countable resources of more than $2,000.

Therefore, all planning related to Medicaid eligibility involves an asset transfer strategy.

> *Risk Management Tip:* The rules and resulting asset transfer strategies are complex. Anyone considering Medicaid eligibility should seek the counsel of an attorney.

NURSING HOME FEARS

Poor planning can lead to denied eligibility, penalties, or both. The Deficit Reduction Act of 2005 requires state Medicaid officials to "look back" at transfers of assets made within five years of the Medicaid applicant's moving to a nursing home, or spending down assets to become eligible for Medicaid before applying for Medicaid coverage.

CAN LIFE INSURANCE OFFSET THE COST OF LONG-TERM CARE?

The sales pitch sounds too good to be true! There are two developing trends in the life insurance and long-term care industry as this book nears publication in early 2014. The two trends are:

1. completing a 1035 exchange from an existing life or annuity policy into a new long-term care insurance policy

2. converting a life insurance policy's death benefit into a living benefit that can pay for senior care, commonly referred to as a long-term care benefit plan

The 1035 Exchange

In my opinion, the best description of this method is in an article posted by Michael Kitces, on his website at www.kitces.com.[11]

Mr. Kitces is a financial planner and suggests this strategy for consumers who are considering how best to fund a long-term care insurance policy. The steps to accomplish this plan require the assistance of a financial planning professional and should be reviewed by an estate planning attorney.

In the simplest terms, the conversion involves surrendering a part of the assets of an annuity or life insurance policy. The money from the surrender is used to purchase a new long-term care policy.

According to those selling the plan, there would be a more favorable tax treatment, because the transfer from a life or annuity policy would be tax-deferred while the tax rules for a qualified long-term care policy treats the benefits as tax-free. It is suggested, by those proposing these types of plans, that since there is no cash value in a long-term care policy, the gain effectively is not just tax-deferred but disappears entirely. Following their logic, there would be no tax due for the benefits if or when they are provided for long-term care.

> [*Risk Management Tip:* Caution! A 1035 exchange plan has the potential of being misrepresented to the buyer. Several suggestions:
>
> 1. Make certain the premium payments are being paid directly to the insurance company, not

---

11 Michael Kitces, "A New Way to Pay for Long-Term Care Insurance with Favorable Tax Treatment," *Nerd's Eye View* (blog), May 8, 2012, www.kitces.com/blog/a-new-way-to-pay-for-long-term-care-insurance-with-favorable-tax-treatment/.

the insurance agent. To my knowledge, no insurance company will sell a long-term care policy on a single-payment basis. A potential scheme would be to overstate the deductibility of the LTC premium and encourage the consumer to use all of the money from the 1035 exchange to buy what is represented as a single-premium LTC policy. An unscrupulous agent could take the premium, keep it all, and then pay the premiums for the policy annually when due. Obviously, once the agent has the single-pay premium, the funds could be used for other purposes.

2. Demand transparency from all parties that would be paid a commission or fee from the purchase of long-term care insurance. Potential tax savings encourage consumers to make the purchase. However, sales fees will be paid to the selling agent, and in some states, fees may also be paid to the financial planner, attorney, and accountant. These costs would be deducted as a part of the premiums. A commission load of 20 percent would significantly reduce the tax savings.]

Long-Term Care Benefit Plan

Converting a life insurance policy's death benefit into a pool of money to purchase senior services is an emerging trend. The process includes the sale of the existing whole life or term life policy to a third party. The ownership of the policy is transferred to the new third-party owner, who will keep paying the premiums and, when the original policyholder dies, collect the death benefit. Also, in the event the third party owner dies prematurely, their heirs inherit the benefits of the life insurance policy when the person dies.

The purchase price of the policy is discounted based upon some percentage of the ultimate death benefit. For example, if the face-value death benefit is $100,000 and the surrender cash value is $10,000, a third-party life settlement company may be willing to pay as much as $30,000 or $40,000 for the policy. This pool of money could then be used to purchase senior services, such as in home health care, assisted living, or independent living care.

There are a number of potential issues that could significantly reduce the net proceeds from the sale of the policy to a life settlement company. These include:

- The health of the seller may reduce the purchase offer. The healthier the seller, the less he or she will be offered, because he or she will be expected to live longer!

- Family members need to be kept informed. Their beneficiary status in the seller's life insurance policy will disappear once the policy is sold to a third party. The new owner will become the beneficiary.

- Policy loans against the insurance policy will need to be cleared by the seller before the policy is sold. Work closely with the insurance company that sold the policy to you. Request an illustration from the insurance company to project any tax liability that may be due upon the payment of the loan from existing cash values.

- Obtaining a second opinion about the advisability of this strategy may be difficult. The life settlement industry was significantly curtailed during the 2008 to 2011 recession. There are very few settlement companies remaining to provide alternative proposals. Therefore, it is expected an independent second opinion will only be available for a fee.

- Mental health of the seller should be validated. Any dementia may cause the sale to be blocked by a family member or be the basis for a declination by the settlement insurance company.

- Tax implications should be considered. There could be a misunderstanding as to the tax consequences of a sale. The cash value of a life policy is generally not taxed unless there has been some taxable event, (such as the sale of the policy to a third party) during the history of the policy. Any amount of money that is received from the sale that exceeds the cash value or the amount of money that had been paid in premium could be subject to a tax.

> [***Recommendation:*** any seller of a life policy should obtain professional assistance from both a tax attorney and an accountant.]

WHAT HAPPENS WHEN THE MONEY RUNS OUT?

Fear of the unknown has been used by agents to sell long-term care insurance. One of the primary fears of the elderly is that they will "run out of money." They also assume and fear that the consequence of running out of money is to be left broke, in an old-age home.

Medicaid is the safety net. If someone has long-term care insurance, and the benefits run out, the federal Medicaid program will provide for the long-term care after the individual's assets are spent down to the required level. It is unfortunate that for many, when the benefits run out, they may be forced to move to another nursing home facility that accepts Medicaid.

At this writing, facilities may opt out of participation in the Medicaid program. This may be a surprise to the consumer who is seeking a place for his or her family member. Even among Medicaid-approved facilities, a loved one may need to pass dementia evaluation criteria for admission. If the loved one fails to pass the evaluation, the facilities may deny admission. For some caregiver children, the elder person may be forced to live with children until such time that a facility can be located.

[Medicaid is intended to be the safety net, but it is no guarantee that the patient's preferred facility will be available. Advance planning will be needed to make the transition as smooth as possible.]

CONCLUSION

Anyone considering the purchase of long-term care insurance should seek multiple proposals and discuss the need for these products with a trusted financial adviser. These products will continue to be aggressively sold to the older people. Also, keep in mind that the numbers often look good if you assume that the person will go into a nursing home for a long period of time. As stated earlier, however, most people are in a nursing home for less than three years.

Long-term care insurance is a tool for some but certainly not the majority of older people. The amount of insurance or existence of insurance should not be the basis for determining when you or a loved one needs long-term care.

The decision to go into a nursing home is best made by the family, rather than being left exclusively to the spouse. A family is faced with many challenges, especially if dementia overwhelms the caregiving spouse.

Often, the husband or wife will go to extraordinary lengths to keep the rest of the family from seeing all of the signs of dementia in his or her spouse. Unknowingly, the spouse can make it more difficult for the loved one to qualify for admission to a facility if he or she covers up these signs. The delay in being assessed can significantly reduce the facility options, because many facilities exclude patients with dementia after they have reached a certain level of dementia.

My primary recommendation is that you make a plan based upon your current assets and the assets that will likely be available later in life. If long-term care insurance is warranted, demand transparent disclosure of all commissions and fees to be paid to third parties, and *always* seek the advice of an independent, trusted advisor to review the proposals.

Ken R. Butler is an entrepreneur and industry leader in the analysis of affluent family and business risk management needs and development of legacy preservation plans.

This book is a general discussion about the subject matter and should not be used in place of legal advice in any state in the United States of America. This book is copyrighted. It shall not be reprinted nor shall portions be reproduced, in any form, by any other party, without the permission of the author.

REFERENCES

Baldwin, William. "Dodge the Long Term Care Insurance Mess." *Forbes*. Accessed January 19, 2014. http://www.forbes.com/sites/baldwin/2013/03/29/dodge-the-long-term-care-insurance-mess/.

Day, Thomas. "Veterans Aid and Attendance Pension Benefit and Long-Term Care Benefits for Veterans." *National Care Planning Council*. Accessed January 12, 2014. http://www.longtermcarelink.net/eldercare/long_term_care_benefits_for_veterans.htm.

Driscoll, Marilee. *The Complete Idiot's Guide to Long-Term Care Planning*. Indianapolis, IN: Alpha Books, 2002.

"Elder Law, Medicaid, Estate Planning, and Long-Term Care: ElderLawAnswers." *ElderLawAnswers*. Accessed January 12, 2014. http://www.elderlawanswers.com/.

Fevurly, Keith R. "Alternatives to Long-Term Care Insurance." *Journal of Financial Service Professionals* 66, no. 6: 61-68 (2012). http://search.ebscohost.com/login.aspx?direct=true&profile=ehost&scope=site&authtype=crawler&jrnl=15371816&AN=83233390&h=NKeUaYcPGksStAc4%2BS

CKLNtkpKv764WBF33eoqd4D%2BRsvrAWKbxMiDhSK%2B%2BvKCHFbeFIbgmmrBeWO3sIaRIQew%3D%3D&crl=c.

Kitces, Michael. "A New Way to Pay for Long-Term Care Insurance with Favorable Tax Treatment." *Nerd's Eye View* (blog). May 8, 2012. www.kitces.com/blog/a-new-way-to-pay-for-long-term-care-insurance-with-favorable-tax-treatment/.

Moeller, Philip. "What You Need to Know about Long-Term Care Insurance." *The Best Life* (blog). *US News & World Report.* February 20, 2013. www.money.usnews.com/money/blogs/the-best-life/2013/02/20/what-you-need-to-know-about-long-term-care-insurance.

Rowley, Stephen F. *The Consumers' Guide to Long-Term Care Insurance.* Bloomington, IN: AuthorHouse, 2004.

Skeeles, James C. "The Nursing Home Dilemma." Publication no. EP 10–12. Ohio State Extension Community Development Fact Sheet. Columbus, OH: Ohio State, 2012.

SUPPLEMENT A
LONG-TERM CARE INSURANCE POLICY COMPARISON WORKSHEET

	A	B	C
General Information	Model		Comments
Telephone number			
Premium grace period	31 days		
AM best financial rating	"A" or better		
Rate guarantee	3 years, then by class		
Legal action requirement	No sooner than 3 years		
Proof of loss	Within 120 days		
Guaranteed renewable	Yes		

KEN R. BUTLER

Return of premium benefit	Not recommended		Usually requires later of reaching age 100 or twenty-fifth policy anniversary
Benefits the Policy Provides			
Years of Coverage Provided	3 Years (min.)		
Total lifetime benefit: continuous care —intermittent care	$165,000 (min.) $165,000 (min.)		
Preexisting condition wait period (Y or N)	Yes, up to 6 months		
Benefits adj. for inflation protection (Y or N)	Yes, but stop at 65		
Tax-qualified policy (Y or N)	No		
Bed hold reservation (Y or N)	Yes		
Adult day care (Y or N)	Yes		
Homemaker services (Y or N)	Yes		
Alzheimer, Parkinson, dementia, and senility covered (Y or N)	Yes		
Trigger: unable to perform number of adult living activities	2		

NURSING HOME FEARS

Annual Premium Amounts			
Premium before riders and discounts	Recommended		
Premium for home health care	Recommended		
Premium for inflation protection	Rec. under age 65		
Premium for non-forfeiture benefit	Not recommended		Costs 10–15% of basic rate
Premium for waiver of premium	Not recommended		
Premium for durable medical equip.	Not recommended		
Worldwide option	Not recommended		
Paid-up benefit	Not recommended		Usually requires later of age 95 or twentieth policy anniversary
Annual Premium after Riders	$500: example		
30 Year Premium: Current $	$15,000: example		
Lifetime Benefit	$165,000		
% 30 Yr Premium to Life Benefit • **Fairly Priced if under 10%**	9%		

63

SUPPLEMENT A
LONG-TERM CARE INSURANCE POLICY COMPARISON WORKSHEET

	A	B	C
Services the Policy Provides	Model		Comments
Nursing home care (Y or N)	Yes		
Assisted living facility care (Y or N)	Yes		
Home health care (Y or N)	Yes		
Respite care benefit (Y or N)	Yes		
Skilled intermediate custodial care (Y or N)	Yes		

Daily & Monthly Policy Limits	Daily/Monthly	Daily/Monthly	
Nursing home care	$150/$4,500		
Assisted living facility care	$150/$4,500		
Home health care/adult day care	$150/$4,500		
Deductible/Elimination Periods (list number of days for each)			
Nursing home care (skilled, intermediate, and custodial)	Not more than 90 days		
Home health care and assisted living	Not more than 90 days		

This is a general discussion about the subject matter and should not be represented as applicable in any state in the United States of America. It shall not be reprinted nor shall portions be reproduced in any form, by any other party, without the permission of the author.

ABOUT THE AUTHOR

Ken R. Butler, CPCU, ARM
3729 Waitley Drive
Richfield, OH 44286

E-mail: ken.r.butler@gmail.com

Mr. Butler, an Associate in Risk Management and a Chartered Property & Casualty Underwriter, graduated from The University of Akron in 1977. He is a leader in the development of "Best Practice" standards for Long-Term Care Insurance programs.

Mr. Butler defines his consultant role as follows:

- Protecting the Family's wealth from erosion due to long-term health care needs

- Developer of "Best Practice" risk management standards and cost controls

KEN R. BUTLER

Vision:

To be forever known as a passionate and independent advocate for the insurance consumer.

www.ingramcontent.com/pod-product-compliance
Lightning Source LLC
Chambersburg PA
CBHW071757170526
45167CB00003B/1063